EASY CLASSICS

FOR THE YOUNG TRUMPET PLAYER

CURNOW® MUSIC

Exclusively Distributed By

HAL•LEONARD® CORPORATION

7777 W. BLUEMOUND RD. P.O. BOX 13819 MILWAUKEE, WI 53213

Order Number: CMP 1063-05-400

EASY CLASSICS FOR THE YOUNG FLUTE PLAYER
Trumpet

ISBN 978-90-431-2377-8

CD number: 19-072-3 CMP

FOR THE YOUNG TRUMPET PLAYER

FOREWORD

EASY CLASSICS FOR THE YOUNG TRUMPET PLAYER is a compilation of solo/recital material from the great masters of musical composition that have been specifically arranged for the Beginner through Early Intermediate instrumental soloist. The soloist will find a wide variety of styles and varying levels of difficulty in this book.

This set includes the Piano accompaniment, the Solo part, and a professionally recorded CD that demonstrates each piece. Use these examples to help develop proper performance practices. There is also a recording of the accompaniment alone that can be used for performance (and rehearsal) when a live accompaniment is not available.

EASY CLASSICS

FOR THE YOUNG TRUMPET PLAYER

CONTENTS

☐ Solo with accompaniment

■ Accompaniment

Ludwig van Beethoven

1. ODE TO JOY

Arr. **Timothy Johnson** (ASCAP)

© 2005 by **Curnow Music Press, Inc.**

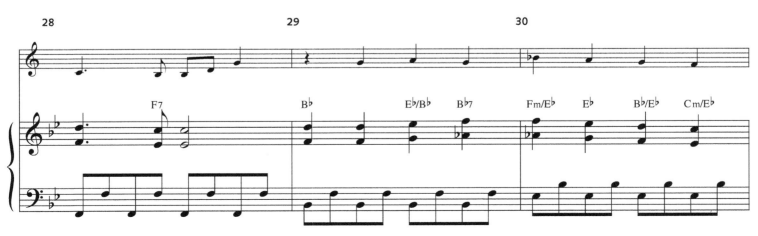

2. FANTAISIE IMPROMPTU

 Arr. **Ann Lindsay** (ASCAP)

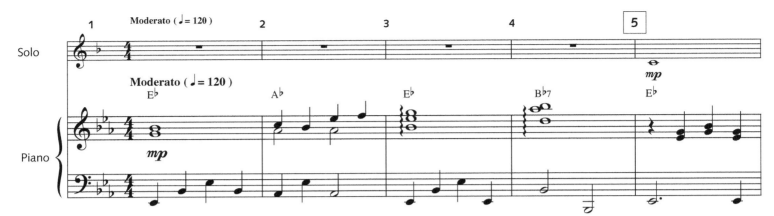

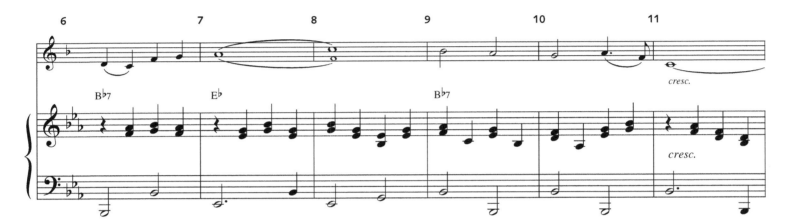

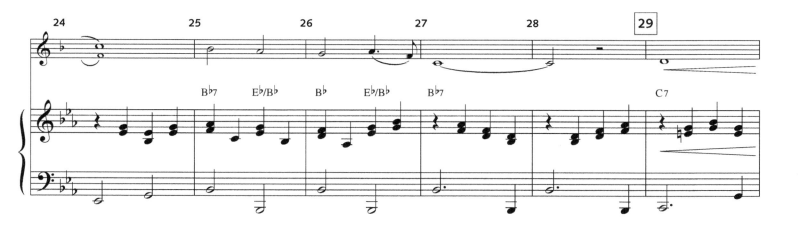

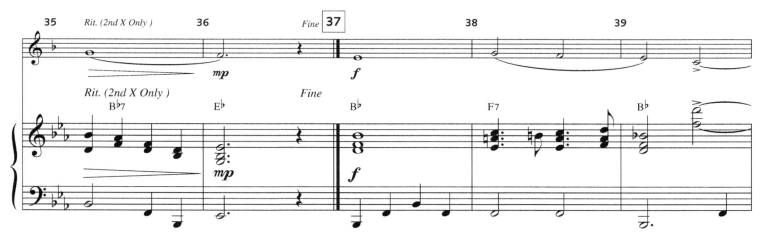

Johannes Brahms
3. FINALE FROM SYMPHONY #1

Arr. **Timothy Johnson** (ASCAP)

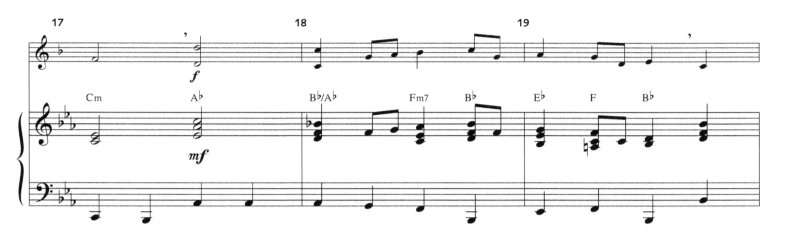

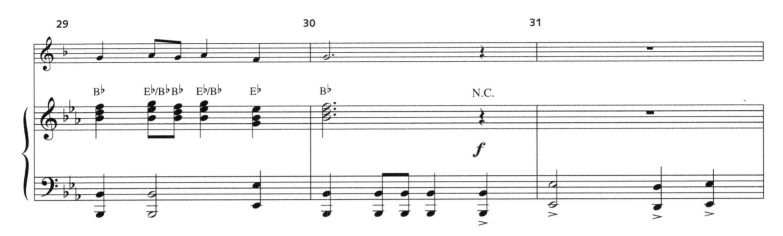

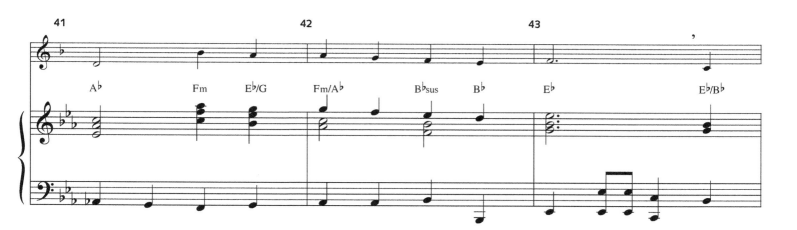

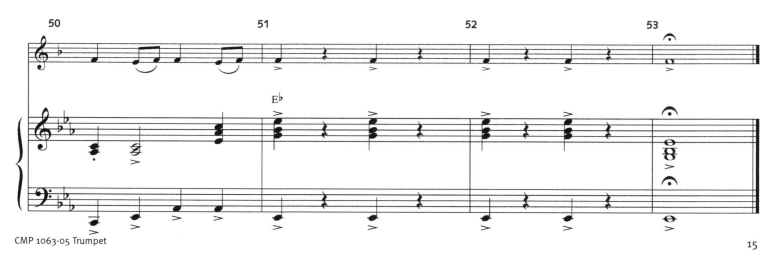

Julius Benedict
4. THE CARNIVAL OF VENICE

Arr. **Mike Hannickel** (ASCAP)

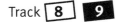

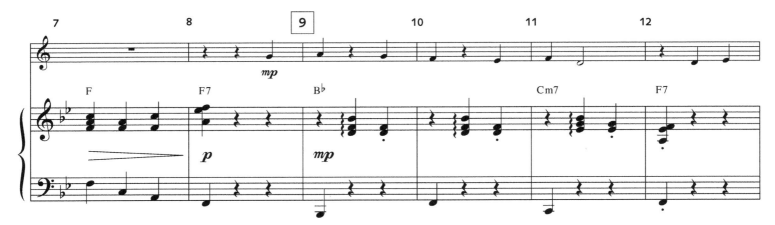
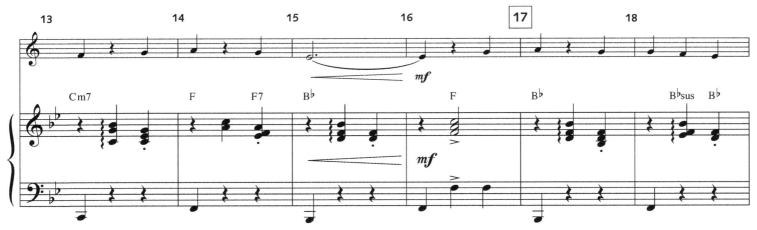
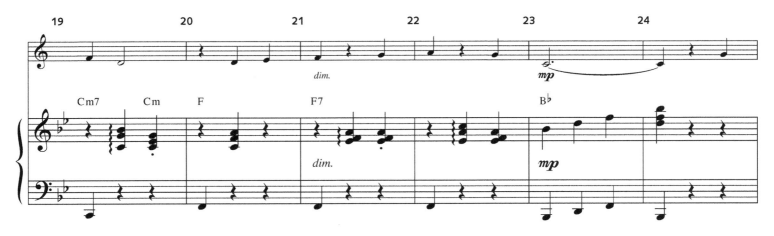

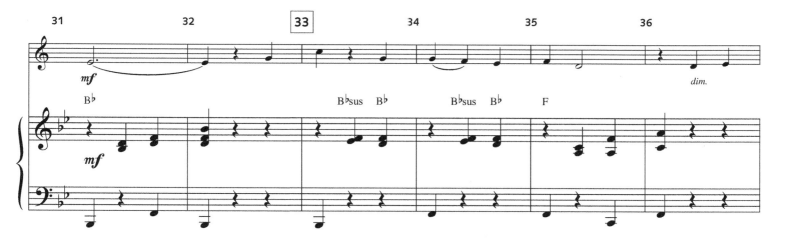

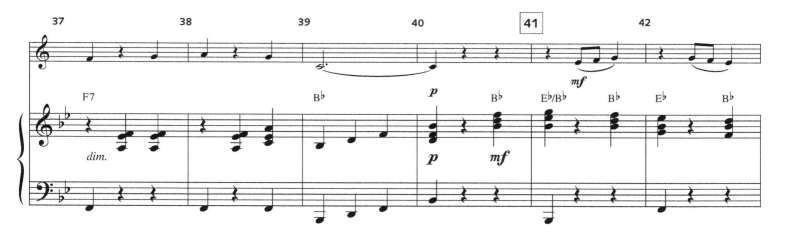

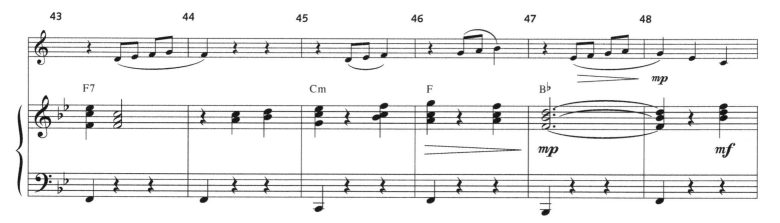

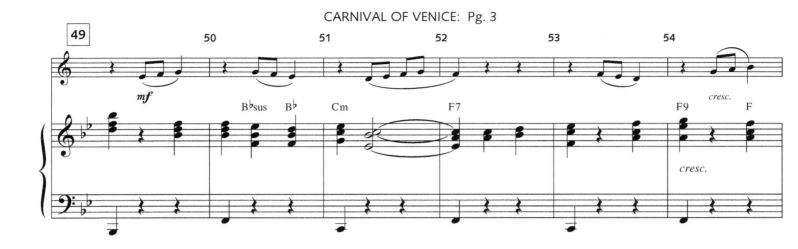

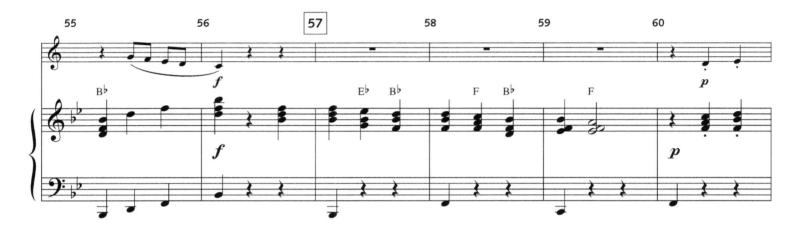

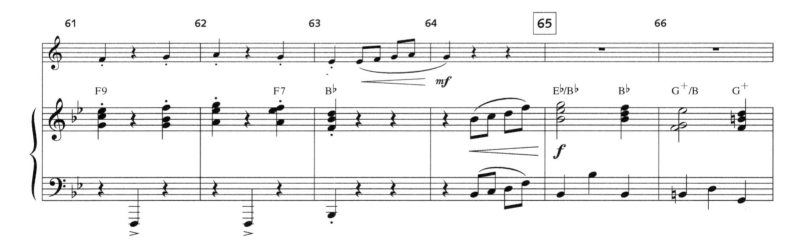

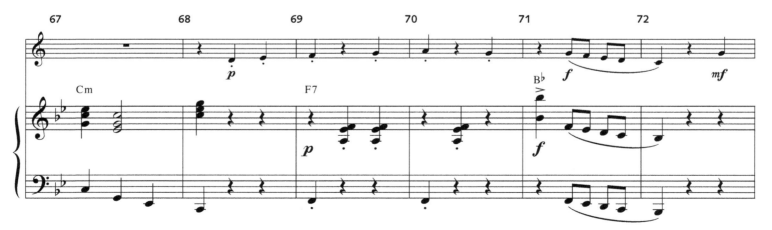

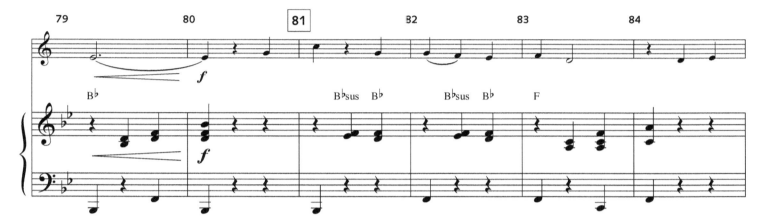

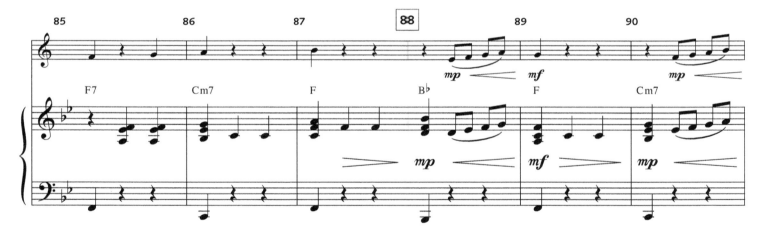

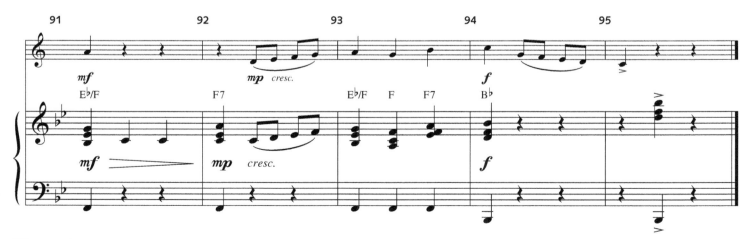

Franz Schubert
5. SANCTUS

Arr. **James Curnow** (ASCAP)

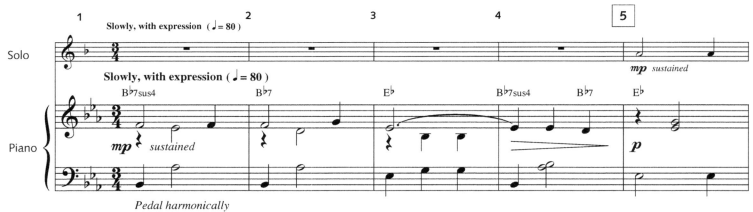

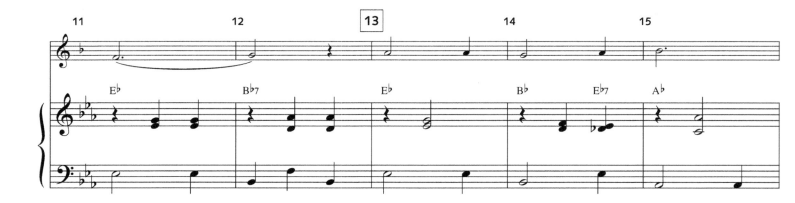

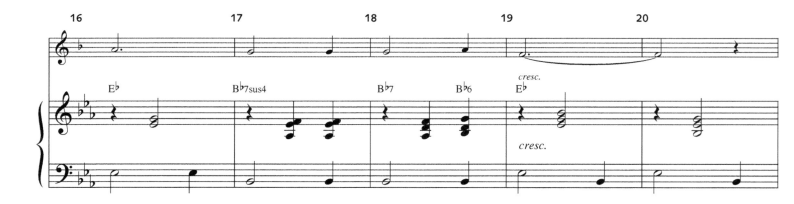

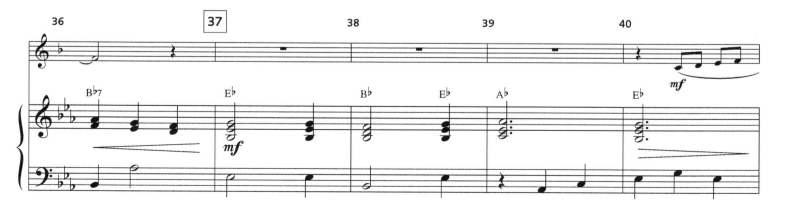

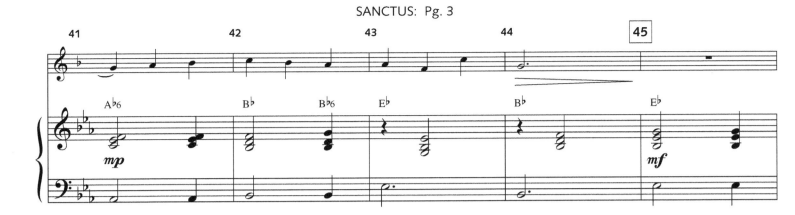

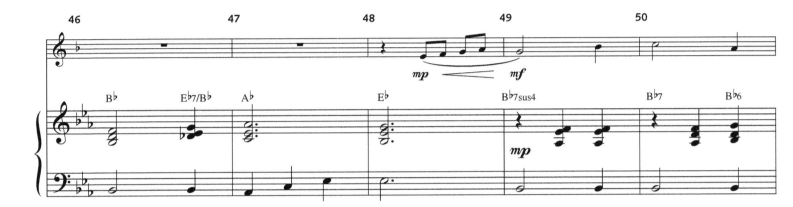

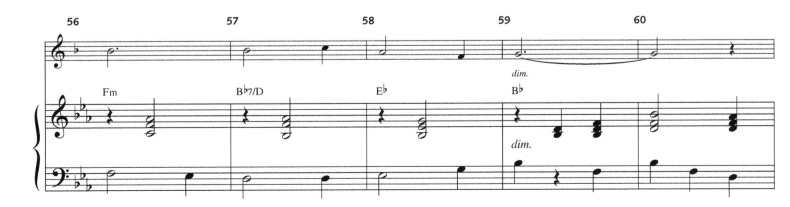

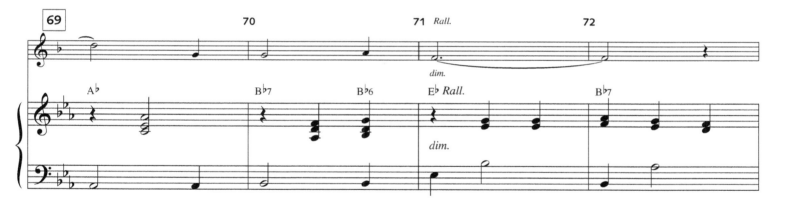

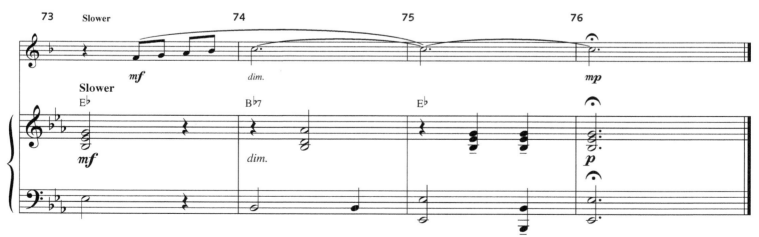

6. HUNGARIAN DANCE NO.6

Arr. Ann Lindsay (ASCAP)

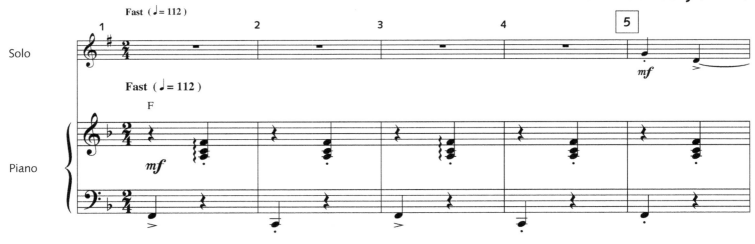

© 2005 by Curnow Music Press, Inc.

EASY CLASSICS
FOR THE YOUNG TRUMPET PLAYER

FOREWORD

EASY CLASSICS FOR THE YOUNG TRUMPET PLAYER is a compilation of solo/recital material from the great masters of musical composition that have been specifically arranged for the Beginner through Early Intermediate instrumental soloist. The soloist will find a wide variety of styles and varying levels of difficulty in this book.

This set includes the Piano accompaniment, the Solo part, and a professionally recorded CD that demonstrates each piece. Use these examples to help develop proper performance practices. There is also a recording of the accompaniment alone that can be used for performance (and rehearsal) when a live accompaniment is not available.

EASY CLASSICS

FOR THE YOUNG TRUMPET PLAYER

CONTENTS

☐   Solo with accompaniment

■   Accompaniment

Ludwig van Beethoven

1. ODE TO JOY

Arr. **Timothy Johnson** (ASCAP)

Frederic Chopin

2. FANTAISIE IMPROMPTU Arr. **Ann Lindsay** (ASCAP)

Johannes Brahms
3. FINALE FROM SYMPHONY #1

Arr. **Timothy Johnson** (ASCAP)

Julius Benedict
4. THE CARNIVAL OF VENICE
Arr. **Mike Hannickel** (ASCAP)

Franz Schubert
5. SANCTUS

Arr. **James Curnow** (ASCAP)

Johannes Brahms
6. HUNGARIAN DANCE NO.6

Arr. **Ann Lindsay** (ASCAP)

W. A. Mozart
7. AVE VERUM CORPUS

Arr. **Timothy Johnson** (ASCAP)

Johannes Brahms
8. WALTZ

Arr. **James Curnow** (ASCAP)

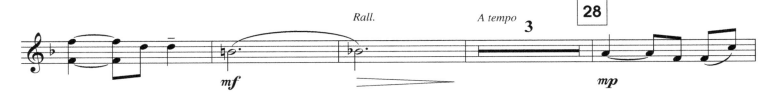

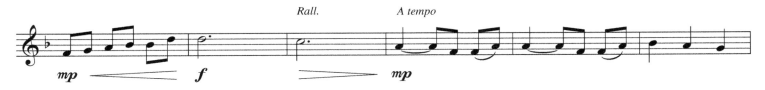

© 2005 by **Curnow Music Press, Inc.**

Edvard Grieg

9. IN THE HALL OF THE MOUNTAIN KING

From Peer Gynt Suite #1

Arr. **James Curnow** (ASCAP)

© 2005 by **Curnow Music Press, Inc.**

Alexander Borodin
Theme from

10. STRING QUARTET #2

"Nocturne"

Arr. **James Curnow** (ASCAP)

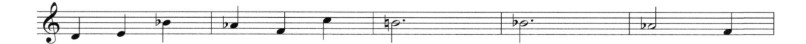

© 2005 by **Curnow Music Press, Inc.**

W. A. Mozart
11. ANDANTE
from LA CI DAREM LA MANO
From Don Giovanni

Arr. **Ann Lindsay** (ASCAP)

Franz Joseph Haydn
12. SERENADE
Opus 3, No. 5

Arr. **James Curnow** (ASCAP)

Moderately slow, in a singing style (♩ = 88)

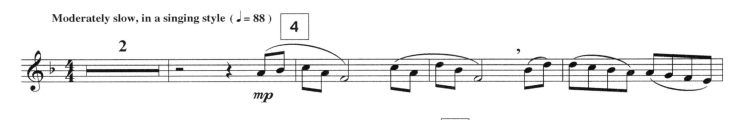

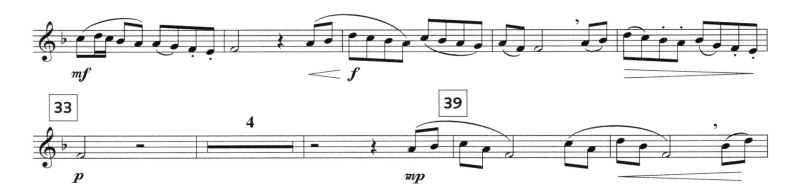

CLASSICS FOR THE YOUNG TRUMPET PLAYER

Music of the great masters: eight wonderful classics in a format that is appropriate for the young instrumentalist: from very easy up to early intermediate levels with a professionally recorded accompaniment CD. Excellent literature for concerts, contests, or home enjoyment. These solos can also be performed with a live band – they are also available as concert band arrangements.

Order Number   CMP 0547-01-400

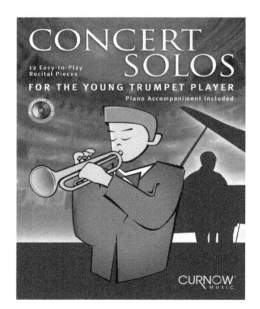

CONCERT SOLOS FOR THE YOUNG TRUMPET PLAYER

High quality solo pieces from very easy up to early intermediate levels with a professionally recorded demonstration/accompaniment CD. Features original compositions by some of today's finest composers for a total of twelve outstanding solos in a wide variety of musical styles. Excellent literature for concerts, contests, church, or home enjoyment. Piano accompaniment included.

Order Number   CMP 1049-05-400

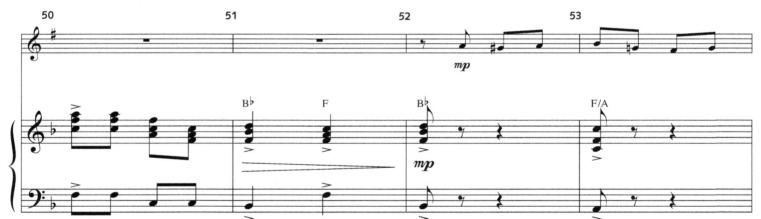

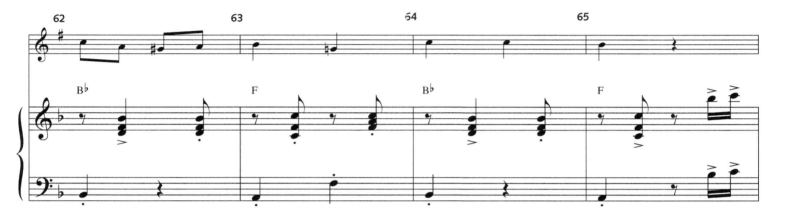

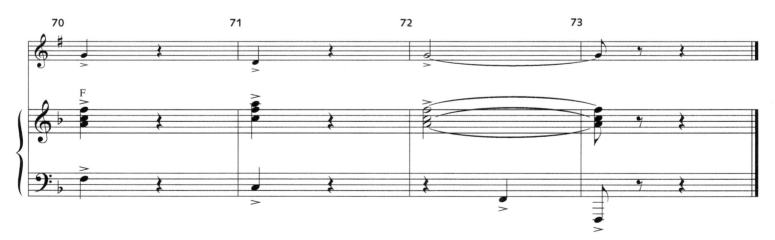

W. A. Mozart
7. AVE VERUM CORPUS

Arr. **Timothy Johnson** (ASCAP)

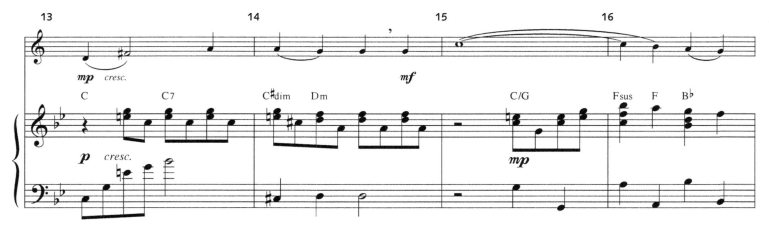

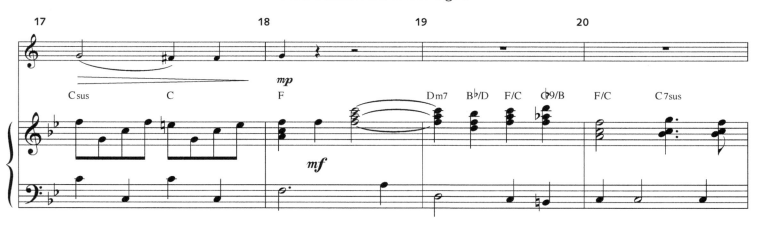

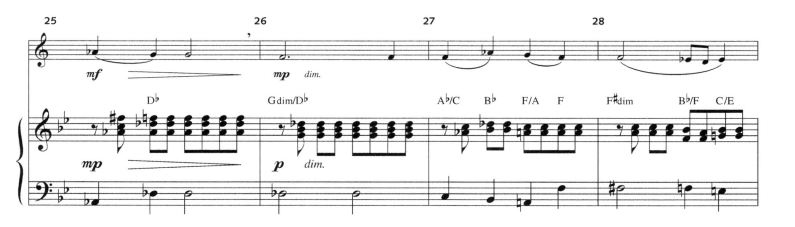

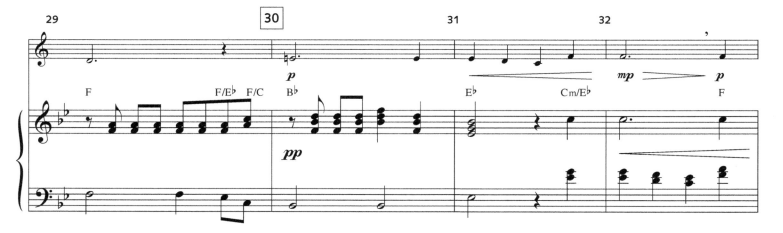

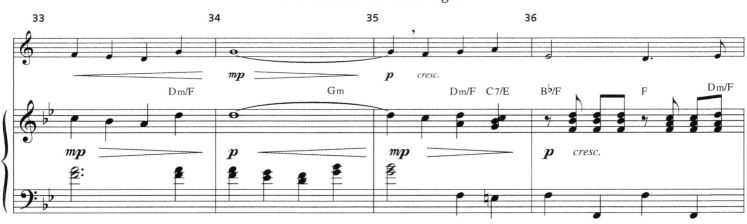

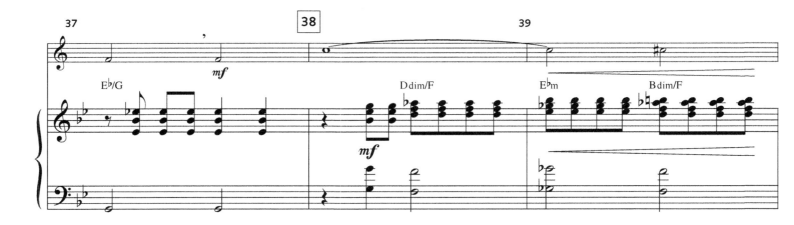

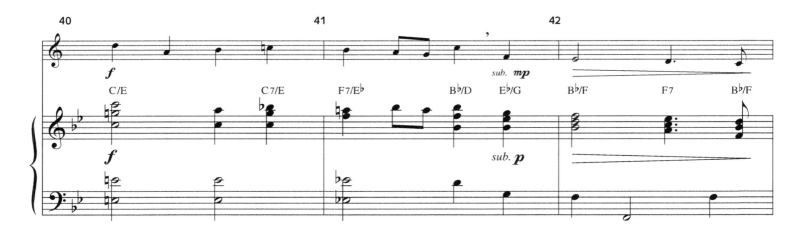

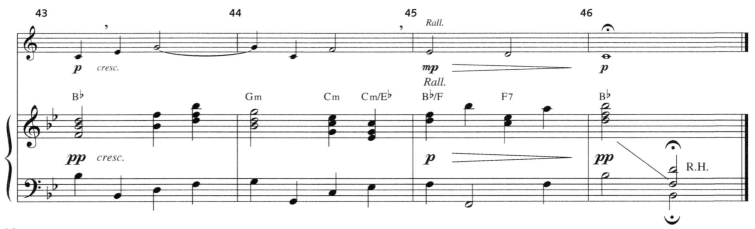

Johannes Brahms
8. WALTZ

Track 16 17

Arr. **James Curnow** (ASCAP)

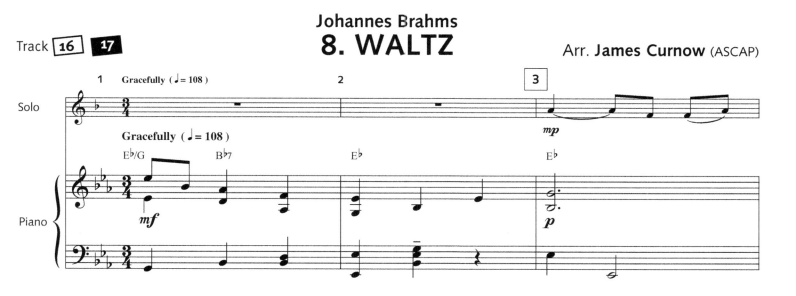

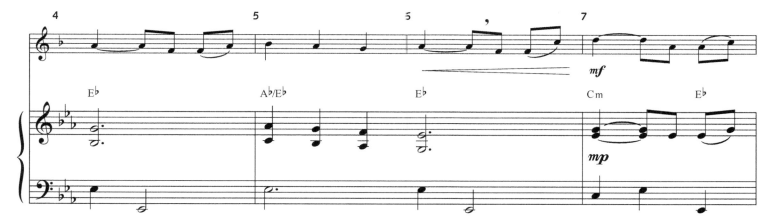

CMP 1063-05 Trumpet

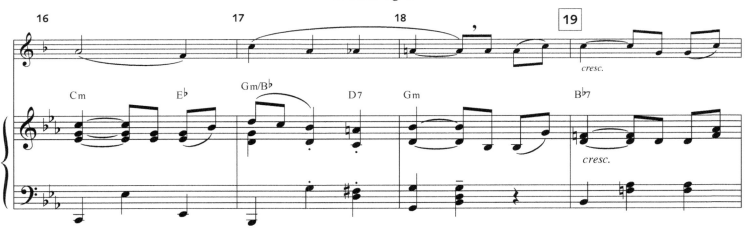

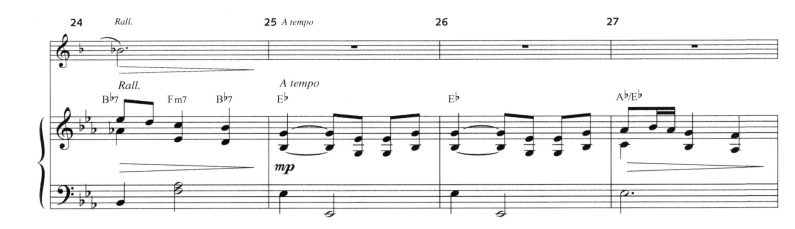

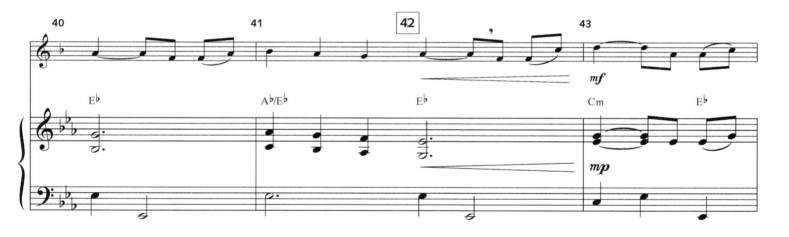

Edvard Grieg

9. IN THE HALL OF THE MOUNTAIN KING

From Peer Gynt Suite #1

Arr. **James Curnow** (ASCAP)

Track **18** | **19**

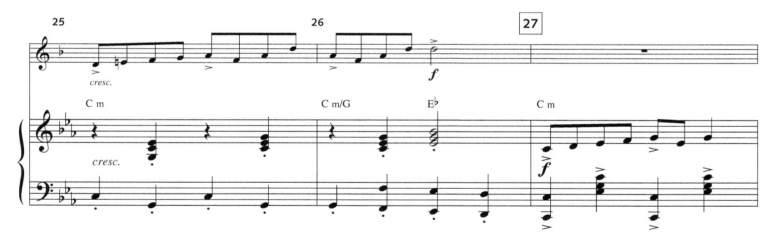

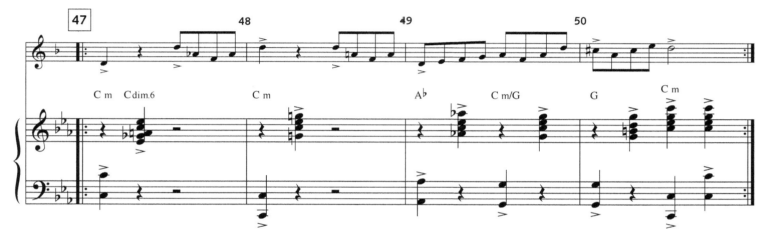

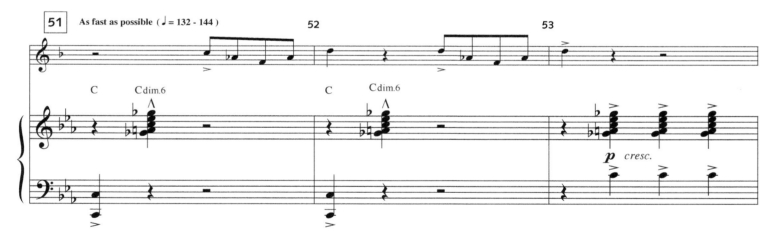

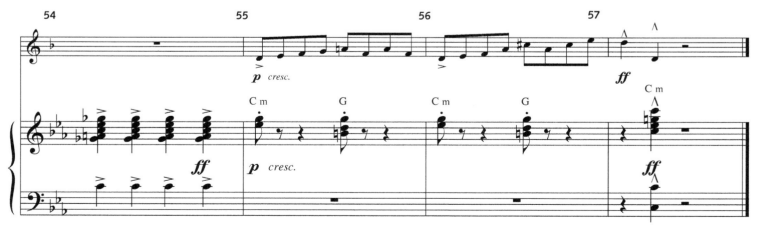

Alexander Borodin
Theme from

10. STRING QUARTET #2

"Nocturne"

Arr. **James Curnow** (ASCAP)

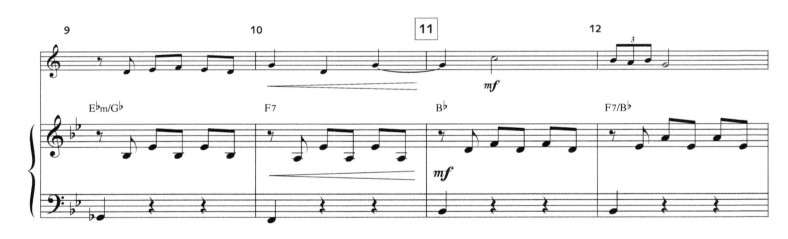

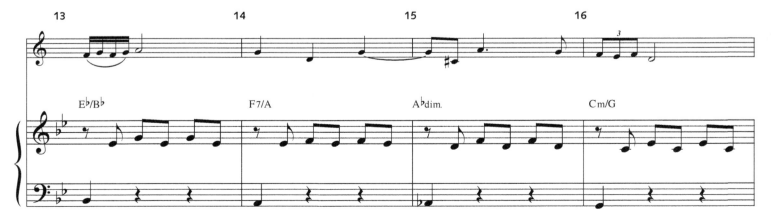

© 2005 by **Curnow Music Press, Inc.**

38

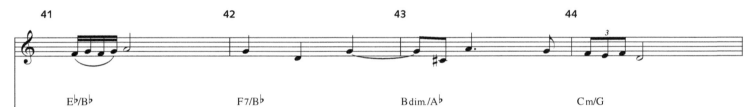

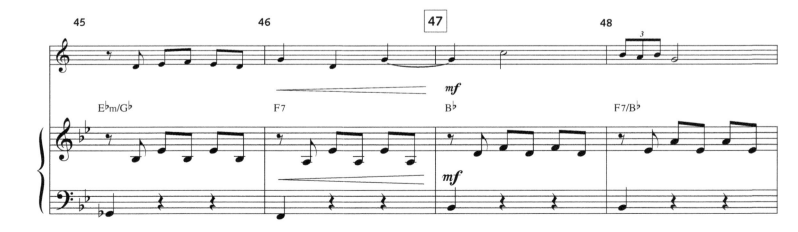

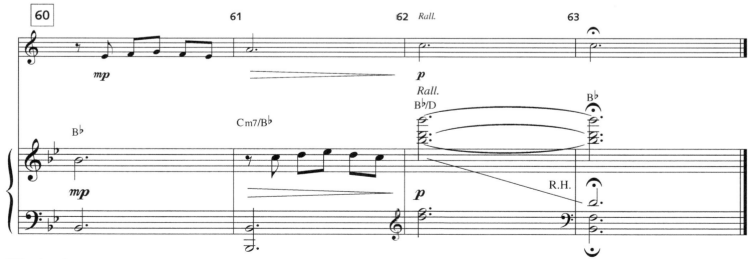

W. A. Mozart
11. ANDANTE
from LA CI DAREM LA MANO

From Don Giovanni

Arr. **Ann Lindsay** (ASCAP)

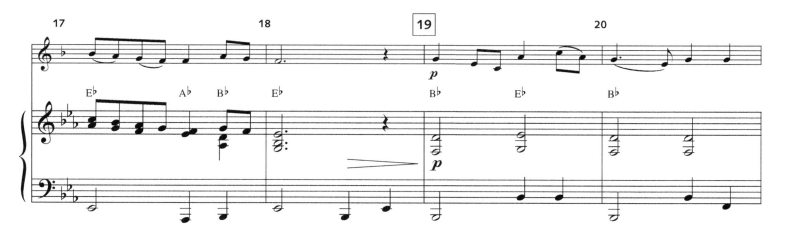

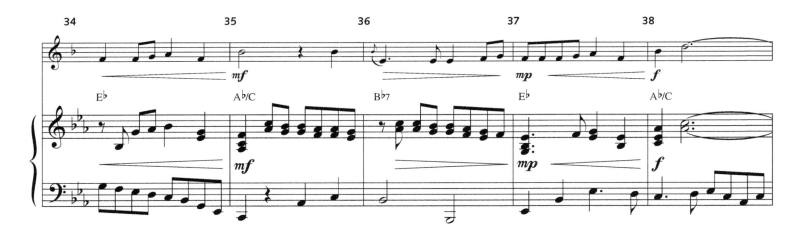

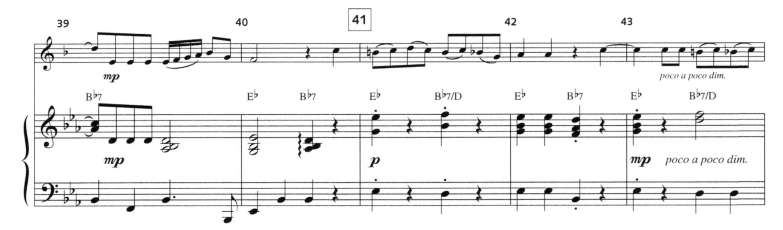

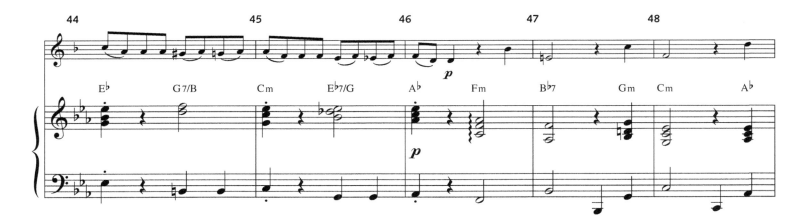

Franz Joseph Haydn
12. SERENADE
Opus 3, No. 5

Track **24** **25**

Arr. **James Curnow** (ASCAP)

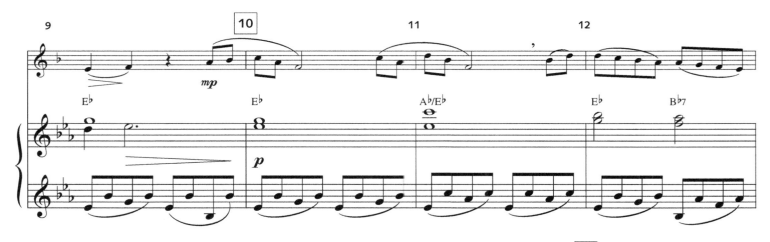

CMP 1063-05 Trumpet

© 2005 by **Curnow Music Press, Inc.**

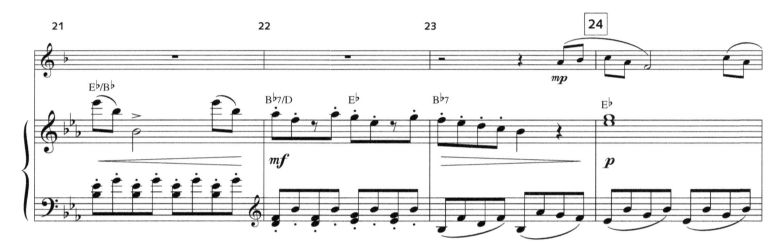

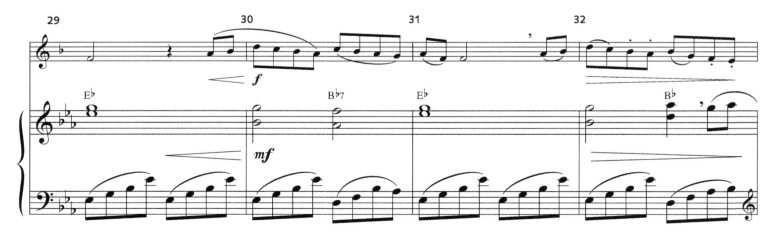

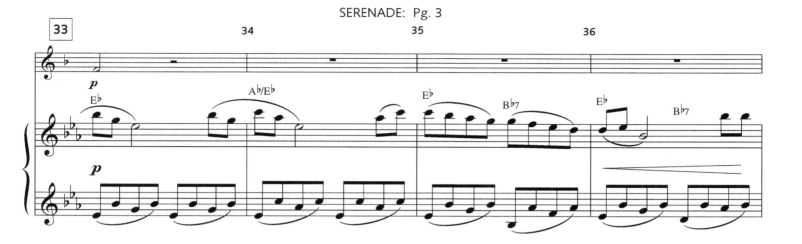

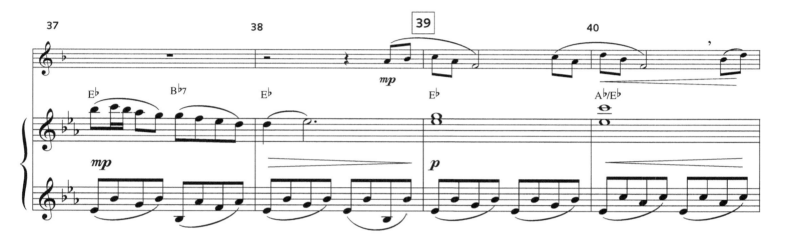

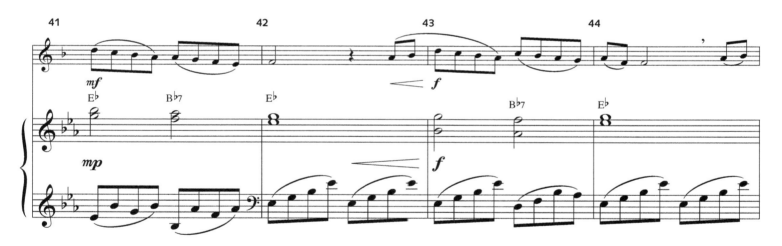

CLASSICS FOR THE YOUNG TRUMPET PLAYER

Music of the great masters: eight wonderful classics in a format that is appropriate for the young instrumentalist: from very easy up to early intermediate levels with a professionally recorded accompaniment CD. Excellent literature for concerts, contests, or home enjoyment. These solos can also be performed with a live band – they are also available as concert band arrangements.

Order Number   CMP 0547-01-400

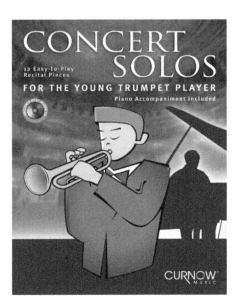

CONCERT SOLOS FOR THE YOUNG TRUMPET PLAYER

High quality solo pieces from very easy up to early intermediate levels with a professionally recorded demonstration/accompaniment CD. Features original compositions by some of today's finest composers for a total of twelve outstanding solos in a wide variety of musical styles. Excellent literature for concerts, contests, church, or home enjoyment. Piano accompaniment included.

Order Number   CMP 1049-05-400